THE DON'T LAUGH CHALLENGE

PRANK-OFF BATTLE

Easter Edition

FAMILY FRIENDLY PRANKS AND PRACTICAL JOKES FOR BOYS, GIRLS, AND KIDS OF ALL AGES

Copyright© 2020 by Bacchus Publishing House
ALL RIGHTS RESERVED. By purchase of this book, you have been licensed one copy for personal use only. No part of this work may be reproduced, redistributed, or used in any form or by any means without prior written permission of the publisher and copyright owner.

GUIDELINES TO PULLING THE PERFECT PRANK

I. The point of a prank is to have fun and get people laughing!

It may not always seem funny to the prankee at the time, but by the time the prank is over it should be funny and lighthearted. Compare:

1. So, we set this church on fire and it burned down. **(NOT Funny)**
2. So, we put 30 'For Sale' signs in front of the school. **(Funny)**

II. Know your Prankee.

If your friend is deathly afraid of clowns, don't dress up as one to scare him/her. If your mom has had a hard day, maybe prank your brother that day. Bottom line, choose your prankee wisely.

III. Fixability.

Anything that causes permanent damage is not considered funny. Do NOT involve any personal property, animals, or unknown people in pranks.

IV. Clean it up!

If you cover someone's room with sticky notes (Hilarious, by the way), you need to also be willing to clean it all up after everyone has had their laughs. If you are not willing to clean, then you might not be such a big prankster afterall, and should stick to something more along the lines of salt cookies instead.

V. Never get into a fight over a prank, just prank them back harder!

If your brother put mayonnaise in your pudding cup, then take time to cool off and start planning your prank off revenge. The best part of any prank is the reaction, so understand that it might come at the cost of yours sometimes.

Now that you've read the Guidelines to Pulling off the Perfect Prank, let's dive into how to play the game!

Directions:

- Face your opponent and decide who is 'Prankster 1' and 'Prankster 2'.

- Starting with Prankster 1, read the prank aloud to your opponent and attempt to complete the prank. If you attempt the prank, you get a prank point. If the prank is successful, Prankster 1 gets an additional prank point! If Prankster 1 does not complete the prank successfully, the prank point is not awarded.

- Once Prankster 1 has completed their pranks, it's Prankster 2's turn. At the end of the round tally up your scores and the prankster with the least points has to complete the End of Round DARE before continuing to the next round!

- Take turns going back and forth between both pranksters as you move through each round, then mark your total prank points at the end of each round!

- After you both complete all 10 Rounds, whoever has the most prank points is crowned the Ultimate Prank Pro!

- In the event of a tie, continue to Round 11 for the Tie-Breaker Round where Winner Takes ALL!

- Have fun and always remember to keep pranks light-hearted!

Let's get started!

➡

DISCLAIMER: Remember, ALL pranks should be fun.
Do **NOT** attempt to harm anyone or damage any personal property!

PRANKSTER 1

THE POLISHED SOAP BAR

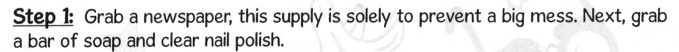

Supplies: Clear nail polish, Bar of soap, Newspaper

Step 1: Grab a newspaper, this supply is solely to prevent a big mess. Next, grab a bar of soap and clear nail polish.

Step 2: Use the clear nail polish to paint a complete top coat on the bar of soap. Wait for the top to dry, then repeat on the bottom of the soap.

Step 3: Clean up all your evidence!

Step 4: Place the bar of soap back on the sink or tub, and wait for someone to get sudsless soap! From experience, you'll most likely hear the frustration of this one, so get your laughs ready!

Prank Point: _____ /2

NO MO TOILET PAPER PRANK

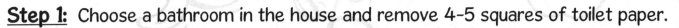

Supplies: Toilet paper, Zip-tie, Safety scissors

Step 1: Choose a bathroom in the house and remove 4-5 squares of toilet paper.

Step 2: Grab the zip-tie and carefully tighten it around the toilet paper roll, but make sure you cut off any excess from the zip-tie, otherwise you'll give it away!

Step 3: Grab your extra toilet paper squares and place them around the roll to cover up the visibility of the zip-tie.

Step 4: Wait with anticipation for the prankee to call out for help on the toilet! You might want to have extra toilet paper on hand!

Prank Point: _____ /2

Continue to the next page for more fun! ➔

PRANKSTER 2

THE FAUX BUG TRAP

Supplies: Fake cockroach or spider, Cup, Sheet of paper, a vulnerable prankee

Step 1: Grab a sheet of paper and write "Don't lift unless you plan to kill it!" on it.

Step 2: Strategically place the cup, flipped upside down, and the paper on the kitchen counter or floor.

Step 3: Hide and watch as your parents get ready to kill a bug that isn't even there! BONUS if you made them jump!

Prank Point: _____ /2

NOT YOUR AVERAGE OREO

Supplies: Oreos, Mayonnaise, Butterknife

Step 1: Grab a pack of Oreos. Separate an Oreo in half and carefully remove the icing layer using a butterknife.

Step 2: Add the mayonnaise in place of the icing. (I recommend doing this step a little bit at a time.)

Step 3: Put the two pieces of the Oreo back together, and clean up the edges, so there's NO evidence!

Step 4: Place the Oreo back in the box and wait for your prankee to get an oreo that isn't so sweet! Muahaha!

Prank Point: _____ /2

Time to add up your points! ➜

ADD UP YOUR POINTS AND SCORE THEM BELOW! THE PRANKSTER WITH THE LEAST POINTS HAS TO COMPLETE THE END OF ROUND DARE!

PRANKSTER 1

/4
ROUND TOTAL

PRANKSTER 2

/4
ROUND TOTAL

ROUND CHAMPION

End of Round

DARE

Go ring your neighbors doorbell and sing 'Jingle Bells' all the way through or until they close the door!

PRANKSTER 1

I SAID RIGHT MEOW!

Supplies: No supplies needed, but you will need some commitment for this one!

Step 1: Replace "now" with "meow" every time you speak, for the rest of the day.

Step 2: When your mom or dad acts confused and asks why you're saying that, act like you have no idea what they're talking about!

Step 3: Try and control your laughter at their confusion!

Prank Point: _____ /2

WORD SEARCH FAIL

Supplies: Sheet of paper, Marker or Pen

Step 1: Get a sheet of paper and create a fake word search by drawing 10 rows of letters across a sheet of paper.

Step 2: Write 7-10 generic words like "Saturday", "Morning", "Winter" at the bottom of the page.

Step 3: Give the sheet to your parents and tell them you've created a word search for them.

Step 4: See how long it takes them to realize there are no words in the letters!

Prank Point: _____ /2

Continue to the next page for more fun! ➡

PRANKSTER 2

ACHOO ON YOU!

Supplies: Water, an unsuspecting prankee

Step 1: Wet your hand by dipping it in warm water, you don't want to have your hand be soaking wet, but enough water to easily flick off.

Step 2: Sneakily, get behind your prankee and pretend to sneeze.

Step 3: As your pretend to sneeze, flick some of the warm water from your hand on the back of their neck!

Step 4: Act shocked when they turn around and apologize profusely! May be hard not to laugh when you see how disgusted they are!

Prank Point: _____ /2

BROWN-E TRICK

Supplies: Brown Paper, Scissors, Pen

Step 1: Grab a sheet or two of brown paper. If you don't have any, color a sheet of paper with a brown crayon or marker.

Step 2: Trace and cut out 5 capital letter E's on the page.

Step 3: Place them on your kitchen counter or on a plastic plate.

Step 4: Go tell your mom/dad you just made a batch of brownies and to go grab one if they'd like! Laugh uncontrollably as they get tricked!

Prank Point: _____ /2

Time to add up your points! ➡

ADD UP YOUR POINTS AND SCORE THEM BELOW! THE PRANKSTER WITH THE LEAST POINTS HAS TO COMPLETE THE END OF ROUND DARE!

PRANKSTER 1

/4
___
ROUND TOTAL

PRANKSTER 2

/4
___
ROUND TOTAL

___

ROUND CHAMPION

End of Round

Smell the feet of everyone in the room and rank them best to worst!

PRANKSTER 1

THE FAKE CAKE

Supplies: Shaving cream, Balloon, Cake pan, Sprinkles (Optional)

Step 1: Grab the shaving cream, a balloon, an empty cake pan, and sprinkles!

Step 2: Blow up the balloon and place it inside the empty cake pan. Cover the entire balloon and the top of the cake pan with shaving cream. Top with sprinkles!

Step 3: Tell your sibling(s) and/or parents you made them a cake.

Step 4: Watch with excitement as they cut their cake and it explodes! Then, RUN!!!

Prank Point: _____ /2

THE SLEEPY FOOD STACK

Supplies: Bread, Cheese, Sleeping sibling

Step 1: Get several slices of cheese and bread. (Optional substitute: Crackers)

Step 2: Sneakily, see how many cheese and bread slices you can stack on your sleeping sibling, before the stack topples over or they wake up!

Step 3: Make sure to take a picture so you can show them when they wake up! I guarantee it'll be hard to keep a straight face!

Prank Point: _____ /2

Continue to the next page for more fun! ➡

PRANKSTER 2

THE NETFLIX SWITCHAROO

Supplies: Netflix account, Remote

Step 1: Login to your favorite TV streaming account. (Optional: Netflix, Disney+, Hulu, etc.)

Step 2: Go into the 'Settings' and change everyone's username and picture.

Step 3: Sit back and watch as everyone tries to figure out which account is theirs or if they are even logged in correctly! Perfect prank to pull on a family movie night!

Prank Point: _____ /2

THE SOUR SURPRISE

Supplies: Water cup, Lemon juice

Step 1: Wait patiently for your friend or family member who is drinking a glass of water to walk away.

Step 2: Sneakily, add a big squeeze of lemon juice and act like nothing happened.

Step 3: Watch as the prankee gets a crazy look on their face to the sour surprise!

Step 4: RUN!!!

Prank Point: _____ /2

Time to add up your points! ➜

ADD UP YOUR POINTS AND SCORE THEM BELOW! THE PRANKSTER WITH THE LEAST POINTS HAS TO COMPLETE THE END OF ROUND DARE!

PRANKSTER 1   /4
———————
ROUND TOTAL

PRANKSTER 2   /4
———————
ROUND TOTAL

———————————

ROUND CHAMPION

End of Round

Yell the alphabet backwards in 30 seconds. If you fail, keep trying until you complete it.

PRANKSTER 1

THE ORIGINAL PRANK CALL

Supplies: Phone, Paper, Pen or Pencil, Sense of Humor

Step 1: Make a short list of goofy trivia questions that don't have a correct answer. (Examples: What color is the number 7? How does a fish fart?)

Step 2: Dial *67 (This blocks your real phone number), then dial your best friend's phone number.

Step 3: Disguising your voice, tell your friend you are calling from a local radio station. Then, instruct them to answer these questions correctly to win tickets to the hottest movie or concert.

Step 4: Ask the questions and try not to laugh! Confess after they've tried to answer your questions and/or start to get frustrated!

Prank Point: _____ /2

IN A PICKLE

Supplies: Cup, Pickle Juice, Thirsty sibling

Step 1: State aloud that you are thirsty and going to get some juice, then offer to bring your sibling a glass of juice, too.

Step 2: After they accept, pour pickle juice into a cup. (Make sure the cup is NOT clear!)

Step 3: Watch as they take a big gulp of your sour drink! They never said WHICH kind of juice!

Prank Point: _____ /2

Continue to the next page for more fun! →

PRANKSTER 2

THE OLE SLIPPERY DOORKNOB TRICK

Supplies: Lotion or coconut oil, Doorknob

Step 1: Grab some lotion or coconut oil from around the house.

Step 2: Pick a door and rub a thin layer of coconut oil or lotion on the doorknob. Carefully, clean up any excess oil not to give it away.

Step 3: Wait for the prankee to try and open the door, but instead have a slippery hand and an unopened door surprise!

Step 4: RUN!!!

Prank Point: _____ /2

THE JELL-O JUICE

Supplies: Jell-O, Cup, Straw

Step 1: You'll want to make your Jell-O mixture the color of another drink, like soda or juice. Once you've chosen your color, add the powder to water and mix well.

Step 2: Add the Jell-O into a regular cup and add a straw. Hide and let cool in your fridge for about 1-2 hours.

Step 3: Bring the drink to a friend or family member and watch the shock when they try to drink their "juice" and nothing comes out!

Prank Point: _____ /2

Time to add up your points! ➡

ADD UP YOUR POINTS AND SCORE THEM BELOW! THE PRANKSTER WITH THE LEAST POINTS HAS TO COMPLETE THE END OF ROUND DARE!

PRANKSTER 1 ___ /4 ROUND TOTAL

PRANKSTER 2 ___ /4 ROUND TOTAL

___

ROUND CHAMPION

End of Round

DARE

Put on your sister's/mom's clothes and do a model runway walk outside as a car drives by!

PRANKSTER 1

THE UNEXPECTED POOP

Supplies: Toilet paper cardboard roll, Water

Step 1: Once the toilet paper runs out, grab the brown cardboard paper roll.

Step 2: Get the cardboard paper roll wet, a little bit at a time, and roll together until it looks like a piece of poop.

Step 3: Leave the fake poop on the toilet seat or on the floor next to the toilet, so the next person to use the bathroom gets an unexpected poop surprise!

Step 4: Wait patiently, until you hear someone scream from finding the unexpected poop! Commence uncontrollable laughter.

Prank Point: _____ /2

THE CEREAL SWITCH

Supplies: 2 Boxes of Cereal OR a Box of Cereal and a Bag of Chips

Step 1: Grab 2 boxes of cereal or cereal and a bag of chips.

Step 2: Switch the components of both boxes/bags, without mixing them together. Put them back in the pantry in their original spots.

Step 3: Watch as someone goes to pour sweet cereal and gets a savory chip or different cereal surprise!

Prank Point: _____ /2

Continue to the next page for more fun! ➡

PRANKSTER 2

SALTY COFFEE, ANYONE?

Supplies: Sugar, Salt, a Coffee Drinker (a.k.a. Mom or Dad)

Step 1: Switch the components of the sugar and salt containers, without mixing them together.

Step 2: The next day while you're eating breakfast, watch as your parents add salt into their coffee.

Step 3: As they take their first sip and make a disgusted face, laugh and tell them the trick, then RUN!

Prank Point: _____ /2

THE BATHROOM BUG SURPRISE

Supplies: Fake bug, Tape

Step 1: Using clear tape, put a fake spider or cockroach onto the top of the toilet seat and tape it down.

Step 2: Open the toilet seat and leave it up, so that your bug is hidden from the next bathroom goer.

Step 3: Wait until someone goes in to use the bathroom, then when they're done wait to hear their scared reaction as they close the seat and see a bug!

Prank Point: _____ /2

Time to add up your points! ➡

ADD UP YOUR POINTS AND SCORE THEM BELOW! THE PRANKSTER WITH THE LEAST POINTS HAS TO COMPLETE THE END OF ROUND DARE!

/4
___
ROUND TOTAL

/4
___
ROUND TOTAL

___

ROUND CHAMPION

End of Round

Call your crush and sing "I love you, you love me" by Barney, to them.

PRANKSTER 1

THE SHOWER SURPRISE

Supplies: Clothespin, Bathtub

Step 1: Grab a clothespin and pick the shower of your choice.

Step 2: Pull the bathtub spout stopper up and use a clothespin to secure the stopper, so it stays upright. (This will make the shower come on unexpectedly when someone turns on the water.)

Step 3: Wait patiently, until your suspect goes for a bath and gets sprayed with the shower! Be sure to wait for their surprised reaction!

Prank Point: _____ /2

NO WATER FOR YOU

Supplies: Masking tape (Optional substitute: Clear tape), Water bottle with spout

Step 1: Unscrew your water bottle top, but be sure to use one with a water spout.

Step 2: Use the masking tape to place a small piece on the underneath side of a water bottle lid.

Step 3: Close the water bottle. When someone goes to drink it, nothing will come out. Wait till you see the look on their faces!

Prank Point: _____ /2

Continue to the next page for more fun! →

PRANKSTER 2

THE INVERTED MOUSE

Supplies: Computer

Step 1: When no one is using the computer, go into the 'Settings' and click on 'Mouse Settings'.

Step 2: One of the options should be 'Invert', which makes the cursor on the screen move in the opposite direction as the handheld mouse. Click 'Invert' and save your changes.

Step 3: Watch as your parents wonder what on Earth is going on with their mouse! Laughter is welcome.

Prank Point: _____ /2

THE CREEPY MIRROR MESSAGE

Supplies: Soap, Towel, Mirror

Step 1: Grab your soap! Liquid will work best, but a soap bar is a solid substitute.

Step 2: Write "I see you" or your own creepy message on the mirror with the soap before someone takes a shower.

Step 3: Then, use a towel to wipe off the residue from the mirror. It doesn't have to be totally clean, but you don't want them to be able to read it before they shower.

Step 4: Listen for the scream when they get out of the shower and read the creepy message on the foggy mirror!

Prank Point: _____ /2

Time to add up your points! →

ADD UP YOUR POINTS AND SCORE THEM BELOW! THE PRANKSTER WITH THE LEAST POINTS HAS TO COMPLETE THE END OF ROUND DARE!

PRANKSTER 1

/4
_____
ROUND TOTAL

PRANKSTER 2

/4
_____
ROUND TOTAL

_____

ROUND CHAMPION

End of Round

Have the person on your right do your hair any way they want, and you have to keep it like that for the rest of the game!

# PRANKSTER 1

TICKED YA!

Supplies: Digital clock, Handy-dandy fingers

Step 1: This one takes a little commitment. Pick a clock in your house that you can change the time on easily (i.e. microwave, oven, even an old school clock on the wall).

Step 2: Change the clock to be one hour earlier than your current time. (So, if it's 12 P.M. you'll want to change it so it reads 11 A.M.)

Step 3: The first time your parents will think it's odd and probably fix the time, but the goal is to change it repeatedly once they fix it, so it will really begin to bug them.

Step 4: Try to do this up until the point they think there is something wrong with the device, and then you can give away your mastermind trick!

Prank Point: _____ /2

THE THIRST TRAP

Supplies: Plastic cup, Water, Thirsty family member

Step 1: Grab a plastic cup, preferably not clear, and fill it up halfway with water.

Step 2: Carefully place the cup of water in the freezer, but be sure it isn't visible to those who open the freezer!

Step 3: The next day, offer to get your sibling or parents a cup of water.

Step 4: Grab the frozen cup of water, bring it to them, and say, "Here's your water, it should be ready in a couple of hours!" - You nailed it!

Prank Point: _____ /2

Continue to the next page for more fun! ➡

PRANKSTER 2

YOU'VE BEEN FRAMED

Supplies: Household photo frames, Patience

Step 1: Go around your house and find all the framed photos.

Step 2: While no one is watching, turn them all around, so they face the wrong direction and you can't see the photo. Repeat to as many photo frames as possible.

Step 3: Wait and see how long it takes for someone to notice! Once they do, try and hold back your laughter as they run around fixing them all!

Prank Point: _____ /2

THE LEVEL UP

Supplies: Blank sheet of paper, Marker, Tape

Step 1: Grab a sheet of computer paper. Using the marker, draw a black circle in the center of the page.

Step 2: Write this on the top of the page: "To level up,", and this on the bottom of the page: "Aim for the hole!"

Step 3: Tape the sheet of paper to the bottom of the toilet lid and close it.

Step 4: Wait for laughter when your prankee goes to the bathroom and sees the challenge! Hope they don't aim... this one might take some cleaning up and explaining!

Prank Point: _____ /2

Time to add up your points! →

ADD UP YOUR POINTS AND SCORE THEM BELOW!
THE PRANKSTER WITH THE LEAST POINTS HAS
TO COMPLETE THE END OF ROUND DARE!

PRANKSTER 1 /4 ROUND TOTAL

PRANKSTER 2 /4 ROUND TOTAL

ROUND CHAMPION

End of Round

DARE

Ask a neighbor for a roll of toilet paper, while doing the potty dance!

# PRANKSTER 1

THE CRACKED PHONE TRICK

Supplies: Prankee's phone, Internet access, High level of sneakiness

Step 1: Get access to your prankee's smart phone without them watching you... Could be a challenge in itself! Once you have it, Google "shattered glass image".

Step 2: Save the photo and set it as the wallpaper, for the phone lock and home screen.

Step 3: When you bring back the phone, fake cry or freak out, and say, "I'm so sorry, I didn't mean to drop it!"

Step 4: Watch as they freak out and try to hold back your laughter!

Prank Point: ____ /2

THE TV REMOTE TRICK

Supplies: Clear tape, Remote, Black marker

Step 1: Grab your clear tape and draw a circle on top of the tape. Color in the circle.

Step 2: Place the piece of tape with the circle over the sensor of the main remote.

BONUS: Tape another identical piece to the sensor on the cable box or TV.

Step 3: Leave your remote back in its original spot. Watch your prankee think the remote is broken. (This works even better when your prankee is excited for their favorite show!)

Step 4: Eventually, let them know of your silly trick and have a laugh together!

Prank Point: ____ /2

Continue to the next page for more fun! ➡

 # PRANKSTER 2

THE MOLDY BREAD BAG

Supplies: *Bread, Black marker*

Step 1: Get a loaf of bread and grab your marker. Draw misshapen circles that look like mold, scattered on the bag.

Step 2: Put the loaf of bread back in the pantry or bread box.

Step 3: Wait to see the reaction of your prankee when they think their bread has gone bad!

Prank Point: _____ /2

THE MINTY SHOCK

Supplies: *Mints, Ice tray, Water, Patience*

Step 1: Grab an ice tray and put water in each cube slot.

Step 2: Then, add a couple mints to each cube. 1-2 should be plenty!

Step 3: Place the ice tray back in the freezer and wait overnight for the ice to freeze.

Step 4: Add a cube to your prankee's soda or juice, and wait for it to melt and make their drink minty! The best part about this prank is the look on their face when their normal drink turns minty fresh!

Prank Point: _____ /2

Time to add up your points! →

ADD UP YOUR POINTS AND SCORE THEM BELOW! THE PRANKSTER WITH THE LEAST POINTS HAS TO COMPLETE THE END OF ROUND DARE!

PRANKSTER 1 — /4 ROUND TOTAL

PRANKSTER 2 — /4 ROUND TOTAL

ROUND CHAMPION

End of Round

Have the person to the left of you do your make-up... blindfolded. If no make-up is present, use kitchen condiments instead!

 # PRANKSTER 1

THE HIDDEN BANANA MESSAGE

Supplies: Banana, Toothpick

Step 1: Grab a banana and a toothpick.

Step 2: By scraping lightly into the banana with the toothpick, write a message. Think "_____ was here" or "Do not eat!"

Step 3: You may not be able to see the message now, but wait a day or two and your super secret message will appear on the banana! Leave it in the kitchen or put it in a siblings backpack for a creepy lunch surprise!

Prank Point: _____ /2

DING DONG!

Supplies: Marker, Paper, Tape

Step 1: Grab a sheet of paper and a marker.

Step 2: Write "Doorbell broken, please yell "DING DONG" really loud!" on the sheet of paper.

Step 3: Tape the paper over the doorbell on the front porch, but make sure no one in the house sees what you're doing!

Step 4: Wait for a visitor and hear them yell! Commence laughter!!

Prank Point: _____ /2

Continue to the next page for more fun! →

# PRANKSTER 2

THE GLASSES TEASER

Supplies: Glasses case, Sheet of paper, Marker

Step 1: Grab a blank sheet of paper and rip off an edge, just big enough that it would fit in a glasses case.

Step 2: Write "JUST" largely on the slip of paper.

Step 3: Place the paper in the glasses case and close.

Step 4: Go give the case to your prankee and say "Just in case". Laugh at their confusion as they open the case to find no glasses!

Prank Point: _____ /2

THE NOT SO HEAVY WEIGHT LIFTING

Supplies: Ziploc bag, Sticky note, Pen, Q-Tip x2

Step 1: Write "Beginner weights: everyone needs to start somewhere!" on the sticky note.

Step 2: Place the two Q-Tips in the Ziploc bag and put the sticky note on the front/top of the Ziploc bag.

Step 3: Tell your prankee you got them some weights to use when they work out and deliver the bag! You did good, laugh it off!

Prank Point: _____ /2

Time to add up your points! →

ADD UP YOUR POINTS AND SCORE THEM BELOW! THE PRANKSTER WITH THE LEAST POINTS HAS TO COMPLETE THE END OF ROUND DARE!

PRANKSTER 1 — /4 ROUND TOTAL

PRANKSTER 2 — /4 ROUND TOTAL

ROUND CHAMPION

End of Round

Create a sandwich by having each person in the room pick an ingredient to add. Once finished, take a bite out of it!

 # PRANKSTER 1

THE SOCK SWITCHAROO

Supplies: Sock drawers x2

Step 1: Pick two prankee's.

Step 2: Be very sneaky and empty their sock drawers.

Step 3: Move their socks to the other prankee's sock drawer to create a switch. (This prank works best if it is done on an adult and a child!)

Step 4: Witness their confusion when they see all their socks are way too big or way too small! Hilarious.

Prank Point: _____ /2

THE FISHING DOLLAR

Supplies: Dollar bill, Long piece of thin string (Optional substitute: Fishing line), Tape

Step 1: Tape the dollar bill to the end of the string securely.

Step 2: Set the dollar bill down on the floor and hide behind a wall with the other end of the string in your hand.

Step 3: When your prankee tries to pick up the dollar, tug the string so quickly that they miss it! Try to fool as many people as you can!

Prank Point: _____ /2

Continue to the next page for more fun! ➡

PRANKSTER 2

THE HIDDEN MONSTER

Supplies: No supplies needed, but sneakiness is encouraged.

Step 1: Hide somewhere in your sibling's room (i.e. closet, under the bed, etc.) right before bedtime. The trick here is not to let anyone, especially your sibling, see where you've gone!

Step 2: Be super quiet while you wait for them to get in bed.

Step 3: Once they're all settled in, jump out and scare them! You might want to run once they see who scared them!

Prank Point: ____ /2

SAY IT, DON'T SPRAY IT

Supplies: Rubber band, Towel (for clean up)

Step 1: Go to the kitchen sink and wrap your rubber band around the lever of the hose faucet, tightly.

Step 2: When the faucet is turned on, water will spray whoever is at the sink in the face!

Step 3: Witness the surprise of the prankee, you might want to run, but don't forget to clean up your mess!

Prank Point: ____ /2

Time to add up your points! →

ADD UP YOUR POINTS AND SCORE THEM BELOW! THE PRANKSTER WITH THE LEAST POINTS HAS TO COMPLETE THE END OF ROUND DARE!

PRANKSTER 1

/4
ROUND TOTAL

PRANKSTER 2

/4
ROUND TOTAL

ROUND CHAMPION

End of Round

DARE

Everything you say for the next 15 minutes must be sung to the tune of 'Happy Birthday'.

ADD UP ALL YOUR POINTS FROM EACH ROUND.
THE PLAYER WITH THE MOST POINTS IS CROWNED
THE ULTIMATE PRANK PRO!

IN THE EVENT OF A TIE, CONTINUE TO ROUND 11
FOR THE TIE-BREAKER ROUND!

PRANKSTER 1 _____
GRAND TOTAL

PRANKSTER 2 _____
GRAND TOTAL

_____
THE ULTIMATE PRANK PRO

ROUND 11

**TIE-BREAKER ROUND
WINNER TAKES ALL!**

PRANKSTER 1

THE CUP BLOCK

Supplies: Red plastic cups

Step 1: While your sibling is in their room with the door closed, stack plastic cups in a pyramid, as high as you can safely build it right next to their door.

Step 2: Once you're done, call them out of their room and watch as they realize they're stuck, unless they pick up all the cups!

Step 3: Laugh while they try to figure out how to get out, and more importantly, how to get to YOU!

Prank Point: _____ /2

THE FEATHER TICKLE

Supplies: Feather, Shaving cream, a sleepy friend

Step 1: Wait for your friend to fall asleep.

Step 2: Quietly, spray shaving cream in their hand.

Step 3: Then, tickle their face lightly with the feather.

Step 4: Laugh hysterically as they smear shaving cream all over their face, while trying to swat away the feather! Best part is the confused face they make when they wake up from this surprise!

Prank Point: _____ /2

Continue to the next page for more fun! ➡

PRANKSTER 2

THE SARAN WRAP SURPRISE

Supplies: Tape, Saran wrap

Step 1: With your sibling's door closed, tightly stretch Saran wrap from one side of the door to the other. The trick here is to make sure it is as high as your sibling's head.

Step 2: Tape each side, so the saran wrap stays in place.

Step 3: Call out for your sibling to come see something amazing.

Step 3: Laugh as they run out of their room and straight into the saran wrap! Looks like they might run after you on this funny prank! BIG SUCCESS!

Prank Point _____ /2

NOT SO JUICY

Supplies: Gallon pitcher, Water, Spoon, Cheese packet from a box of Mac n' Cheese

Step 1: Take the cheese powder packet from the box of mac n' cheese and pour it into a pitcher.

Step 2: Fill the pitcher with water and use your spoon to mix well.

Step 3: Place the pitcher in the fridge and wait for someone to make a glass of this interesting drink! Be sure to try not to laugh when they almost spit out their mac n' cheese juice!

Prank Point _____ /2

Time to add up your points! ➡

ADD UP ALL YOUR POINTS FROM THE PREVIOUS ROUND. THE PRANKSTER WITH THE MOST POINTS IS CROWNED THE ULTIMATE PRANK PRO!

 **PRANKSTER 1** ___/4
ROUND TOTAL

 **PRANKSTER 2** ___/4
ROUND TOTAL

_____

THE ULTIMATE PRANK PRO

End of Round

**Crack an egg over your head.
Oh yeah, and clean up the mess, too!**

Check out our

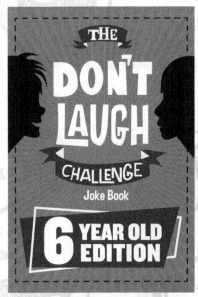  

 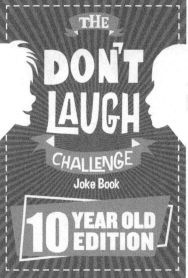 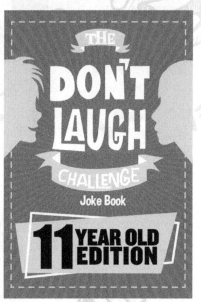

Visit us at
www.DontLaughChallenge.com
to check out our newest books!

other joke books!

If you have enjoyed our book, we would love for you to review us on Amazon!

Made in the USA
Middletown, DE
21 March 2020